Ebay Gold

The Secret to Earning Hard Cash on Ebay

Don Loyd

Ebay Gold
The Secret to Earning Hard Cash on Ebay

Books From DreamMaker Press

Creating Wealth for Women
Creating Wealth in Declining Real Estate Markets
Creating Wealth Manual
The Cure for Declining Income
Move in Now – Buy Later
Taking Back Your Life
How to Use a Buy/Sell Analysis
I Can Be an Author
Creative Real Estate Your Way to Riches
The Right Real Estate Exit Strategy
How to Buy Your First Home
Developing Attitudes for Life Change
How to Improve Your Credit Rating
Living the Dream
A Practical Guide for the FSBO
Mortgage Magic
Retirement Recovery Guide
The Business of Real Estate Investing
The Six Figure Real Estate Broker
The Secret to 7 Figures

Disclaimer

Note from Don Loyd

Is it possible for you to work at home and help provide the income necessary to provide for your family?

If you will do your homework and keep moving forward, and embrace an "I can do this" mindset, my experience indicates you can.

Owning your own business does take more effort and patience than going to work at a fast food restaurant, bank or office job. However, the returns are far more gratifying. The rewards are directly linked to the effort you place into it. Better yet, you have the potential to profit every day – day in and day out.

I believe it's important to have several streams of income. Ebay is a good place to start moving forward. In this book, we're going to go over everything you need to know to get started in your own private online Ebay business. By the time you finish this book, you will know how to invest, how to price your inventory, and what to expect in income.

Let's get started.

Table of Contents

1. Introduction to Ebay Profits

If you've ever read an article about eBay, you will have seen the kinds of incomes people make - it isn't unusual to hear of people making thousands of dollars per month on eBay.

Next time you're on eBay, take a look at how many PowerSellers there are: you'll find quite a few. Now consider that every single one of one of them must be making at least $1,000 per month, as that's eBay's requirement for becoming a PowerSeller.

- **Silver** PowerSellers make at least $3,000 each month,
- **Gold** PowerSellers make more than $10,000,
- **Platinum** PowerSellers make more than $25,000, and
- **Titanium** PowerSellers make at least a whopping $150,000 in sales every month!

The fact that these people exist gives you the idea of the income possibilities here. Most of them never set out to even set up a business on eBay - they simply started selling a few things, and then kept going.

There are plenty of people whose full-time job is selling things on eBay, and some of them have been doing it for years now.

Ebay Gold

Can you imagine that? Once they've bought the stock, everything else is pretty much pure profit for these people - they don't need to pay for any business premises, staff, or anything else. There are multi-million pound businesses making less in actual profit than eBay PowerSellers do.

Even if you don't want to quit your job and really go for it, you can still use eBay to make a significant second income. You can pack up orders during the week and take them down to the post office for delivery each Saturday. There are few other things you could be doing with your spare time that have anywhere near that kind of earning potential.

What's more, eBay doesn't care who you are, where you live, or what you look like: some PowerSellers are very old, or very young. Some live out in the middle of nowhere where selling on eBay is one of the few alternatives to farming or being very poor.

eBay tears down the barriers to earning that the real world constantly puts up. There's no job interview and no commuting involved - if you can post things, you can do it.

Put it this way: if you know where to get something reasonably cheaply that you could sell, then you can sell it on eBay - and since you can always get discounts for bulk at wholesale, that's not exactly difficult. Buy a job lot of something in-demand cheaply, sell it on eBay, and you're making money already, with no set-up costs.

If you want to dip your toe in the water before you commit to actually buying anything, then you can just sell things that you've got lying around in the house.

Search through that cupboard of stuff you never use, and you'll probably find you've got a few hundred dollars' worth of stuff lying around in there! This is the power of eBay: there is always someone who wants what you're selling, whatever it might be, and since they've come looking for you, you don't even need to do anything to get them to buy it.

So you want to get started on eBay? Well, that's great!

There are only a few little things you need to learn to get started. Read on!

EBay 101

EBay works in a very simple manner. There are no hidden secrets for you to learn before you start selling online and there are no hidden costs credited to you. All you have to do is list an item for sale on eBay. The item can be as simple as a watch or as elaborate as your lost uncle's stamp collection. You can either accept bids on your item in an auction format or you can offer buyers the "Buy It Now" option that allows them to buy your item immediately.

PowerSellers quickly learn what sells on eBay and what doesn't. When you find an item, or a group of items, that sell well you'll want to learn to utilize your selling techniques as much as possible.

The online auction method is simple to understand. The opening bidding price begins at a price that you determine for a certain number of days, chosen by you. During this time buyers place bids on your item. At the end of the listing period the highest bidder wins the item.

The "Buy It Now" method of selling simply means that the first buyer who is willing to pay the price you are asking for your item wins the auction.

There are some things that you should know and understand about the selling process at eBay. These important points will be discussed in a later chapter.

EBay provides you with all the tools you need to begin your selling your items immediately. EBay has fine-tuned the art of the online auction by trial and error.

They want to ensure your success and have developed a step-by-step formula for you to register, list your items, maintain your eBay account, and make a profit.

EBay's step-by-step formula includes:

- Decide what you want to sell and do the appropriate research to become knowledgeable about your item.
- Register at eBay and get a seller's account.
- Accurately and concisely create an eBay "listing" for the item you are selling.
- Receive payment from the buyer after your item sells.

EBay's online virtual marketplace has all the tools you need to sell successfully and make a profit. The simplicity of eBay makes it easy for you sell confidently in a stress-free online atmosphere.

---

2. Getting Started

It's easy to start selling at eBay since the process is easy and smooth to understand and implement….and it costs you very little money to get started.

One of the most significant things to note about selling on eBay is that there is little financial risk involved to get you started. Most new businesses require large amounts of money to cover start-up costs such as rent and distribution.

There are really only a few things that you need to become a PowerSeller on eBay:

- products to sell
- a digital camera so that you can take pictures of the items that you're selling an upload them to the eBay website
- a computer
- the enthusiasm to become an eBay PowerSeller and increase your annual income

You'll want to make sure that you have enough room in your house to accommodate the items that you're going to be selling. You'll need to have room set aside not only to store these items but also a space set aside where you can manage the shipping of these items. If your goal is to be a huge eBay PowerSeller you might want to eventually find a space to rent so that you can sell your items in large quantities.

Ebay Gold

There are many sellers on eBay since the process of signing up is so simple. Becoming an eBay PowerSeller is just one step away from being a seller who sells only the occasional item. PowerSellers make multiple sales each month and earn high profits from these sales.

Getting started selling at eBay is as simple as registering your name, or your business name. There are some details that you'll need to include in your registration as a seller, such as where you are located and how you plan on shipping your sold items.

Your goal as an eBay PowerSeller should be to look as professional as you can so that buyers take you seriously and learn to trust your reputation. Setting up an "online" shop is one way that you can gain a more professional outlook among the many sellers that can be found on eBay.

There are several different options available at eBay that will help you to make a good impression on buyers. You don't want buyers to think of you as just another eBay seller and pass you by for a more professional seller.

When you first start selling your items on eBay you'll find that there is a learning curve as you find out what works for you and what doesn't. The important thing is to be flexible so that you can make changes to the way that you sell in your favor.

3. Creating Your Account

All types of people and businesses are using eBay to sell their products. This includes the stay-at-home mom who is supplementing her family's income by selling craft products to large companies such as IBM who are seeing huge profits by selling online through eBay.

When you sell items on eBay you can reach a large number of customers all around the world. There are many benefits to selling on eBay. Some of these legal and financial benefits include:

- The low cost of registering at eBay.
- The ability to have fast and secure transactions with your buyers.
- Tax laws that are clearly defined.
- Accounting advice that even an amateur can follow.
- Low advertising costs.
- Free advertising tools.

There are many books that have been published that show you how successful you can be selling on eBay. This is a great market niche itself, to focus on the sale of items that show others how to sell, what to sell, and what to sell it for. With so many benefits of selling on eBay more and more people are taking advantage of the opportunity. Make sure that you're one of the successful sellers by knowing all of the legal and financial angles of the eBay selling process.

The sellers who fail are often the ones who remain blind to the legal side of selling online through eBay.

Studies show that the most successful sellers on eBay operate businesses that are well organized and maintain perfect financial records of each and every transaction that they do both through eBay and with their wholesalers.

The first thing that you will have to do in order to sell on eBay to is register. There are several reasons why you first have to register on eBay. These include:

- EBay requires a certain amount of personal information from you. This is to keep the eBay site secure.
- EBay requires that you register with them before you can begin selling an item or bidding on other saleable items.
- Registration will provide you with updates on the latest eBay information and deals.

Registration at eBay is easy. All you have to do is follow the steps laid out for you. You will be required to provide your name, address, phone number, and a valid e-mail address. Many eBay PowerSellers choose to use a business name for their online transactions. You'll want to include this business name in your eBay registration.

The next step needed for registration is your online user ID. This is the ID by which you will be known as both a buyer and seller. Make sure to choose an ID name that sounds businesslike and professional. You will not want to come up with a cute name only to want to change it to something more sophisticated at a later date. Choose a password that is easy for you to remember.

Once you have completed the first two steps you simply have to check your e-mail for confirmation of your registration. You will then need to set up a seller's account. You will be asked to provide a valid credit or debit card as well as provide your banking information. This is necessary so that when you start selling your items eBay has accurate and legitimate information about how and where you will be accepting payment.

EBay also needs your banking and credit information so that they can bill you appropriately for the small fees owed to them for any listing fees and commissions. Any personal information collected by eBay is done through a secure system so you do not have to worry about security issues.

The registration process takes only a few minutes for you to complete. Make sure your credit card and banking information is accurate and up to date to avoid confusion and error later.

During the registration process at eBay you'll be required to provide information about yourself and the items that you're selling.

One of the things that you'll want to remember is to always keep the information in your seller profile current. Not only does eBay need to have this current information, sellers want to see that your information is accurate since it lends you a high degree of professionalism.

Ebay Gold

Your email address: When you first register with eBay you'll be need to use a current email address for the registration process. If you change your email address it's not necessary to register again. You want to maintain the status that you've built up as a successful seller on eBay by simply notifying eBay of your email address change.

There is a "Change of Email Address" form that you can fill out and return to eBay that makes the change easy and fast. It's important that you don't register with your new email address because when you do you risk losing the information and data that correlates with your old email address.

Should you mistakenly reregister with a new email address it can take eBay administration up to two weeks to merge the data from the old address to the new one. In the event that you do register again with a new email address you can contact eBay at ukemerge@ebay.com to let them know.

Your User ID: You can change your User ID at any time by using the "Change User ID" form. Your User ID is an important aspect of your eBay account. It's a way for buyers to identify you easily, especially when you're relying on repeat sales from the same buyers. You don't want to take the chance of buyers not finding you by changing your User ID. This is why it's important to create a User ID that you know is right for your business when your first register with eBay so that you avoid these changes.

Your User ID should be a reflection of you and your business as opposed to a cute user name. Remember that buyers are going to identify you by this User ID so you want to be as professional as possible.

Your eBay password: Your password is your access to your eBay account so you'll want to remember it and protect it. If you want to change your password at any time you can use the "Change Password" form on the eBay website. There is also a "Forgot Your Password" form that you can fill out if you forget what your password is.

You'll receive notification in your email of how you can change your password so that you can access your eBay seller's account.

Your present password will stay valid until you change it, so if you forget your password you won't be able to access your account until you fill out the "Forgot Your Password" form and make the password change and respond back to eBay with replying email.

Your account information: When you want to make any other account changes that include information about your account or yourself, you can contact eBay by using the "Change Your Registered Information" form.

This form will allow you to make any changes to your account that you need eBay and buyers to know. Keep in mind that any changes may take a day or two to be implemented on your account information page. Plan your changes accordingly so that you let your buyers see what you want them to see.

Other administration features: There are other administration features at eBay that you should be aware of so that you can become familiar and proficient with the selling process. The more experienced and comfortable you are moving around the eBay website the more you can focus on the selling of your products and the promotion of your business.

If you're looking for a certain feature of eBay, and can't seem to find it, don't hesitate to contact them by email to find the appropriate place where you need to look.

Some of the other administrative features that you can find on eBay include:

- Feedback Forum: The Feedback Forum is filled with information about your eBay transactions. This information is available for other eBay users to see.
- My eBay: This eBay feature allows you to view your current, and historical, selling and bidding information. This is handy feature to have since you can find out in one viewing what you've sold and what you've bidding on if you're buying something from another seller.
- About Me: The "About Me" feature of eBay lets you provide any other information to eBay registered users that you want them to know. This can include personal or business information.

EBay administrative services are there to make your selling experience as easy as possible and so that your business can succeed.

Take advantage of these administrative services whenever you can so that you build a solid and positive relationship between eBay and yourself.

4. What to Sell

First off, you need to know what it is you're going to sell: what's your specialty?

You'll do far better on eBay if you become a great source for certain kind of products, as people who are interested in those products will come back to you again and again. You won't get any loyalty or real reputation if you just sell rubbish at random.

When you think about what to sell, there are a few things to consider. The most important of these is to always sell what you know. If you try to sell something that you just don't know anything about then you'll never write a good description and sell it for a good price.

You might think you're not especially interested in anything, but if you think about what kind of things you usually buy and which websites you go to most often, I'm sure you'll discover some kind of interest. If all else fails mention it to your friends and family: they'll almost certainly say "Oh, well why don't you sell..." and you'll slap your forehead.

Out of the things you know enough about, you should then consider which things you could actually get for a good enough price to resell, and how suitable they would be for posting. If you can think of something of that you're knowledgeable about and it's small and light enough for postage to be relatively cheap, then that's great!

Don't worry if you think the thing you're selling is too obscure - it isn't. There's a market for almost everything on eBay, even things that wouldn't sell once in a year if you stocked them in a shop. You'll probably do even better if you fill a niche than if you sell something common.

5. Tax and Legal Matters

If you earn enough money, you should be aware that you're going to have to start paying tax - this won't be done for you. If you decide to sell on eBay on a full-time basis, you should probably register as a business.

Everyone Should Own a Business—Let Me Tell You Why

First, if you own a business you are already a step ahead of the crowd. You can enjoy tax advantages that most people you know can't, unless they too, have a business. In real terms, that means you have more spendable money. You can start writing off several expenses, including vacations, with before-tax dollars. How you would like to be able to do that? If done correctly, it is doable.

Second, if your plan is to quit your day job and become a full-time in you business, you can more easily qualify for traditional financing on a new home if you've been in business for 2 years.

Third, if you have your own business you can set up a self-directed 401k retirement plan when appropriate. The reason that's important is you can loan money from your 401K (charged points and fees) and buy property in that retirement account name while deferring or eliminating taxes on the growth of the fund. You can amass huge sums of money quickly and pay lower taxes at the same time if done properly, all of the time gaining protection for your property under a corporation or LLC. That is the short list. There are many advantages you have when you form a company.

How Do I Set Up a New Business?

I have talked about the importance of protecting your personal assets and separating them through an appropriate business structure, and I have mentioned some other great advantages to being self-employed that clock-punching employees do not have.

Hopefully, the information has not been too boring. Remember, you don't need to be an expert in law or accounting, but it is always important to know enough to be able to ask the right questions to the experts.

You now have a pretty good understanding of the foundation of starting your own business. Now, you just need to execute. This is what you need to do next.

Step One. Decide what business you want to operate.

Step Two. Decide on a business structure. Talk to your attorney and tax advisor about the type of business structure best for you. I think most new businesses should do well if they are set up as an LLC or a Corporation. Recently, there has been new developments regarding Limited Liability Companies and your definitely need to talk to an expert.

Step Three. Choose a name. Give serious thought to the name you use. Make yourself a list of the possibilities. When you have weighed all the pros and cons and have a "short list" left, you need to find out if that name is available for use. Search your state government website to determine how to check if the name is available. Also search to see if you can get an URL for webpage use.

Step Four. Once you decide on a company name, you must register the name with the state. Every state has different forms for registering a business name. Locate the website for your state government, locate the search field, and locate the field to register your business name. Follow the instructions. While there, search through other new business information on their site. If you intend to do business across multiple states or across the country, you may want to consider filing your company's name with the federal government.

Step Five. You need a federal employer identification number (EIN) for banking purposes. It's very easy to obtain. You can also use your Social Security Number, but getting an EIN is easy and if you do any business at all you will need one at some point. So, go ahead and get it now. Go to http://www.irs.gov/ where you can either proceed with the online application, which is very easy, or call the 800 number. If you call, they are very friendly and helpful. They will give you an EIN while you are on the phone. Be sure to write it down and keep it safe.

Step Six. You now need a LLC or Corporation Operating Agreement. You can get your attorney's advice and have him prepare the document. You can also purchase a prepared one online, at one of the local office supply or specialty bookstores, or you can also borrow one from a friend and retype it. In any event, you need an agreement that describes how you will operate your business. If you are setting up an LLC or Corporation for the first time, spend the money and talk to an attorney. It will be money well spent. Be sure to have annual meetings so you fulfill the basic legal requirement. You don't want a judge later on declaring your LLC a shell and not really a business as a result of a minor oversight.

Now you have the basic steps in setting up your company. One final thought . . . why not take your spouse to Maui for your Annual Meeting next year? You can do that and write part of the cost off your income tax. Isn't that great?

6. Prepare Yourself

There are going to be ups and downs when you sell on eBay. Don't pack it in if something goes a little wrong in your first few sales: the sellers who are successful on eBay are the ones who enjoy it, and stick at it whatever happens.

Anyone can sell on eBay, if they believe in themselves - and if you do decide it's not for you, then the start-up costs are so low that you won't really have lost anything.

If you're ready to start selling, then the next thing you need to know is the different auction types, so you can decide which ones you will use to sell your items.

7. Listing Your Items

There are some simple basics that you should know about listing your items for sale on eBay. The more items that you list the more experienced you'll become in knowing how to write descriptions to entice buyers to take a longer look at the item that you're selling than the items of other sellers.

The first thing that you need to do is find items that you want to sell. For your first few selling attempts choose items that you yourself like so that you can create a listing that you can relate to.

Find similar items that are for sale on eBay so that you get a good idea of how much the item is worth, what other sellers are selling it for, and what category it best fits into. To find items that are similar to the one that you're selling use the following steps:

- Use the "Search" button at the top of the eBay webpage.
- Select the "Advanced Search" and type in key search words.
- Choose the "Completed Items Only" option.

You'll quickly have a listing of items that were for sale on eBay but are now ended so that you can see what items are popular and what didn't sell.

Once you have your item ready to sell you're ready to begin listing it. The steps that you'll need to complete, in the following order, are:

- Select the format that you want to use to sell your item.
- Choose the best category for the item.
- Write a title that catches the eye of buyers.
- Write a complete description of the item making sure to include all the specifics such as measurements and condition.
- Include photos of the item that you're selling in the listing.
- Let buyers know where you live.
- Use some of the promotion tools available at eBay to promote the item.
- Include the payment that you'll accept for the item as well as information about shipping and packaging.

Be creative and step outside of the box. You need to establish new ways of marketing the items that you're selling. Take time to examine your competitors on eBay so that you know what they're doing and what you have to do better.

Once you are registered and have set up your seller's account you are ready to list the items that you want to sell. This is known as your eBay "listing". Your goal is to create a listing that is sensational and stands out from other listings. The secret to making money on eBay is to attract as many bidders as possible. There are several different sections that you can complete to create an eBay listing that is perfect for the item that you are selling. These include:

- Selecting a selling format that is right for you. Do you want to use the online auction format or set a definite fixed price for your items? You may want to experiment with several items and use a different selling format for each one. Keep track of which selling format works best for which items. The "Buy It Now" option may work wonderfully for one particular item but for another item it may be more advantageous to sell using the online auction format. Once you have experimented with a few items you will soon know what selling format to use for which of your sellable items.

- Choose the right category for your items. You will want to find the category or categories that best define the items you are selling. This is so that target buyers are able to easily and quickly find your item. If you are unsure about what category to choose for you items it is wise to play it safe and list them in more than one category.

- Write a descriptive title for your items. Choose words that define what you are selling and that will appear in any search that a buyer might try on eBay. Remember that you are competing with many other PowerSellers to get the attention of buyers and earn money.

   Your title is important because eBay's search engine works by reading the title line. You should try and use some key words in your title line for these search purposes. Clearly identify the item. If possible mention a brand name. The more information contained in your title line the more bidders you will attract to your listing.

- Description of your items. This is your opportunity to be creative and promote your item. A description should be written in some type of logical order. You should: (a) describe what the item is, (b) include the title, (c) include the artist, author or manufacturer of the item, (d) indicate identifying marks or other identifying information, (e) describe what the item is made of, (f) list the size and dimensions, (g) describe the condition of the item, and (h) include any special history or features that you think the buyer should know. It is also important to include one line in your description that encourages buyers to e-mail you with any questions.

- Use pictures. People like to see exactly what they are bidding on. EBay makes the process of including pictures in your listings an easy process.

  Pictures will attract buyers to your items. If you are posting more than one photo use your most informative picture first, one that includes all the features of your item. Take the time to get the lighting in the photo right and the setup of the item correct so that you are taking a top-quality picture. Remember that a picture is worth a thousand words and will sell your item.

- Price. Decide what price you want to establish for the items you are selling. Determine whether you are using the online auction format or are using the "Buy It Now" option. You will also want to decide how long you want your listing to run. It is important to carefully determine what price is best for the item you are selling. Take the time to look at similar items that are selling on eBay.

Research your competitors and see what they are doing. If you want to sell crystal vases, for example, you should take a look to see at what price other vases are being sold and at what prices they are listed.

It is important that you research similar items so that you know what price to charge and if there is a market for what you want to sell. This step is vital since you may discover that you can't compete with current sellers on price or there is simply no market for what you have to offer.

- Indicate your payment and shipping preferences. You should offer as many payment options for the buyer as possible, including credit cards. The more payment options that you offer potential bidders the more attention your item will attract. This will ensure you success as an eBay PowerSeller.

Your eBay listing needs to be an attention-getter so that you give the buyer a reason to linger and take a longer look at the item that you are selling. Remember to check your spelling and avoid spelling mistakes. Misspelling of words is unprofessional and may make the difference between selling your item and having the listing expire without a sale.

Try to avoid using words in your eBay listing such as "rare" or "amazing". These are fluff words and will not convince buyers that they need your item just because it is amazing. Buyers will make their decision about the rarity of your item based on the concise and accurate information that you provide in you listing description.

When you are satisfied with the way the listing looks for your item you are ready to place the listing on eBay for buyers to bid on. Make sure to take a look at the way your listing looks online after you have completed the online steps. Make revisions to your listing if you're the least bit unsure about how it looks. It may take you a few tries for the first few items that you list but the effort will be well worth it.

EBay has administrative services that will help you create an item listing that give you the impact that you need to make those sales. In fact, eBay will write your item descriptions for you if you lack the confidence or the talent to do so yourself. You may want to take advantage of this administrative feature until you get the hang of being a PowerSeller on eBay.

If you decide to sell your items through an online shop you'll have to pay a bit more for the listing price but this also means that there will be more advantages to you as a seller. You'll be able to display all of the items that you have for sale at a lost cost that allows you to focus your business expenses in other areas, such as advertising or the purchase of products to sell.

If you're going to be selling your items through an online shop the first 30 days will be free so that you can determine if this format is right for you and what you're selling. Many buyers will take a look at all of the items that a seller has for sale. You want to make it as easy for the buyer as possible to find out all they can about what you're selling and who you are.

8. EBay Sellers Checklist

Being a seller is a lot of responsibility, and sometimes you might feel like you're not doing everything you should be. This simple checklist will help you keep on top of things.

Have you found out everything you possibly could about your items? Try typing their names into a search engine - you might find out something you didn't know. If someone else is selling the same thing as you, then always try to provide more information about it than they do.

Do you monitor the competition? Always keep an eye on how much other items the same as or similar to yours are selling, and what prices they're being offered at. There's usually little point in starting a fixed price auction for $100 when someone else is selling the item for $90.

Have you got pictures of the items? It's worth taking the time to photograph your items, especially if you have a digital camera. If you get serious about eBay but don't have a camera, then you will probably want to invest in one at some point.

Are you emailing your sellers? It's worth sending a brief email when transactions go through: something like a simple "Thank you for buying my item, please let me know when you have sent the payment".

Follow this up with "Thanks for your payment, I have posted your [item name] today". You will be surprised how many problems you will avoid just by communicating this way.

Also, are you checking your emails? Remember that potential buyers can send you email about anything at any time, and not answering these emails will just make them go somewhere else instead of buying from you.

Do your item description pages have everything that buyers need to know? If you're planning to offer international delivery, then it's good to make a list of the charges to different counties and display it on each auction.

If you have any special terms and conditions (for example, if you will give a refund on any item as long as it hasn't been opened), then you should make sure these are displayed too.

Have you been wrapping your items correctly? Your wrapping should be professional for the best impression: use appropriately sized envelopes or parcels, wrap the item in bubble wrap to stop it from getting damaged, and print labels instead of hand-writing addresses. Oh, and always use first class post - don't be cheap.

Do you follow up? It is worth sending out an email a few days after you post an item, saying "Is everything alright with your purchase? I hope you received it and it was as you expected."

This might sound like giving the customer an opportunity to complain, but you should be trying to help your customers, not take their money and run.

Ebay Gold

Being a really good eBay seller, more than anything else, is about providing genuinely good and honest customer service. That's the only foolproof way to protect your reputation.

9. Reputation Value

Your eBay reputation is everything you are on eBay - without it, you're nothing. Your reputation is worth as much as every sale you will ever make.

If you've ever bought anything on eBay (and the chances are you have), then think about your own behavior. Buying from a seller with a low feedback rating makes you feel a little nervous and insecure, while buying from a PowerSeller with their reputation in the thousands doesn't require any thought or fear - it feels just like buying from a shop.

A Bad Reputation Will Lose You Sales.

In fact, a bad reputation will lose you almost all your sales. If someone leaves you negative feedback, you will feel the pain straight away, as that rating will go right at the top of your user page for everyone to see.

Who's going to want to do business with you when they've just read that you "took a month to deliver the item", or that you had "bad communication and sent a damaged item"? The answer is no-one.

Your next few items will need to be very cheap things, just to push that negative down the page. You might have to spend days or even weeks selling cheap stuff to get enough positive feedback to make anyone deal with you again.

It's even worse if you consistently let buyers leave negative feedback - once you get below 90% positive ratings, you might as well be invisible.

You Can't Just Open a New Account.

Besides eBay's rules about only having one account, there are far more downsides than that to getting a new account. You literally have to start all over again from scratch.

You won't be able to use all the different eBay features. Your existing customers won't be able to find you any more.

Your auctions will finish at a lower price because of your low feedback rating. Opening a new account is like moving to a new town to get away from a few people who are spreading rumours about you: it's throwing out the baby with the bathwater.

A Good Reputation Will Get You Sales.

When a PowerSeller tells me something, I tend to believe them. They can be selling a pretty unlikely item, but if they guarantee it is what they say it is, then I trust them - they're not going to risk their reputation, after all. This is the power of a reputation: people know you want to keep it, and they know you'll go to almost any lengths to do so.

This is true even to the point that I would sooner buy something for $20 from a seller I know I can trust than for $15 from someone with average feedback. It's worth the extra money to feel like the seller knows what they're doing, has all their systems in place and will get me the item quickly and efficiently.

10. Successful Selling System

So you want to be a successful seller with your own eBay business, do you? Here's a simple, ten-step path to eBay enlightenment.

Step 1: Identify your market.

Take a while to sit and watch for what sells and what doesn't out of the items you're interested in. Any market research data you can collect will be very useful to you later on. You'll probably see the 'sweet spots' quite quickly - those one or two items that always seem to sell for a good price.

Step 2: Watch the competition.

Before you invest any money, see what the other sellers in your category are up to, and what their strategies are. Pay special attention to any flaws their auctions might have, because this is where you can move in and beat them at their own game.

Step 3: Find a product.

Get hold of a supplier for whatever it is you want to sell, and see what the best rates you can get are - don't be afraid to ring round quite a few to get the best deal. If the eBay prices you've seen are higher than the supplier's, then you're set.

Step 4: Start small.

Don't throw thousands at your idea straight away - get started slowly, see what works and what doesn't, and learn as you go. Remember that it's very cheap to try out even the craziest ideas on eBay, and who knows, they might just work!

Step 5: Test and repeat.

Keep trying different strategies until you find something that works, and then don't be ashamed to keep doing it, again and again. The chances are that you've just found a good niche.

Step 6: Work out a business plan.

A business plan doesn't need to be anything formal, just a few pages that outline the market opportunity you've spotted, your strategy, strengths and weaknesses of the plan and a brief budget. This is more for you than it is for anyone else.

Step 7: Invest and expand.

This is the time to throw money at the problem. Buy inventory, and start spending more time on your business. Set a goal number of sales each week, increasing it each time.

Step 8: Make it official.

Ebay Gold

Once you've made a few thousand dollars worth of sales, you should really register yourself as a business. Don't worry, it's not expensive or hard to do - a lawyer is the best person to help you through the process.

Step 9: Automate.

You'll probably find that you're writing the same things again and again in emails or item descriptions. This is the time to give up on the manual method and turn to automated software that can create listings for you, and respond to completed auctions and payments with whatever message you provide.

Step 10: Never give up.

Even when it looks like it's all going wrong, don't stop trying until you succeed. If you keep working at it then you'll almost always find that you make a real breakthrough just when things are starting to look desperate.

Once you get into the swing of things, you might start thinking that you should quit your job and take up eBay selling part time. But it's not always as easy as that - there are all sorts of factors that you need to consider. The next email will weigh up the case for and against taking up eBay full-time.

10. Powerselling 101

As explained earlier in this guide, PowerSellers are the people on eBay who've made it, recognizable by the little 'PowerSeller' badge next to their name. You've probably seen these people around - and to succeed on eBay, you want to think the way they do.

eBay gets to decide who can be a PowerSeller and who can't, and they have strict requirements. To get in at the minimum PowerSeller level, you must have a feedback rating of at least 100 (minimum 98% positive) and sell at least $1,000 worth of items every month for three months in a row.

There are different levels of PowerSeller membership as you sell items of greater value: $1,000 total is bronze, $3,000 is silver, $10,000 is gold, $25,000 is platinum and $125,000 is titanium.

If PowerSellers ever fail to meet the required amount of sales, or their feedback falls below 98% positive, then they lose their PowerSeller status. In short, the only people who get to be

Ebay Gold

PowerSellers on eBay are the people who have been successful for a good while, and are on track to stay that way.

11. The Shop and the Marketplace

This is the most important part of understanding how PowerSellers think. They don't see what they're doing as being some random bazaar, or a hobby - instead, they see themselves as a business.

Put it like this. If you run a stall in a marketplace, the chances are that you have a general area of business, but you mostly just sell whatever you can get your hands on that week.

If your dodgy buddy got his hands of a job lot of something at a discount, then that's what you'll be selling. This might be fun - and when you have a good week, you'll have a really good week - but it's no way to run a real business in the long-term.

PowerSellers think far more like shops. They sell the same things again and again, every week - regular stock for regular customers. They do 'boring' business things like keep inventories and budgets. They know what they're going to be selling, how much they buy it for and how much they expect to sell for. Just like a real shop, there can be hard times sometimes, but their income is stable and their business can grow slowly.

The best advice I can give you on thinking like a PowerSeller is this: <u>don't take long-term risks for short-term gain</u>. Look after your reputation, manage your selling properly, provide good customer service and the rewards will come to you in due course. And you'll get a little badge next to your name that makes people trust you more!

One possibility that you might have realised so far is what eBay can do for any other businesses you might have. Remember, millions of people visit eBay every day - why keep everything separate when you're starting to tap into that kind of power?

12. Product Categories

Some people think it's easy to choose the right eBay category, and often it is. Sometimes, though, it might not be quite clear exactly what to go for.

Why is it Even Important?

Plenty of people use the category system to find items, when they're not looking for something specific. If your item is listed in the wrong category - or you've just given up and listed it in 'Everything Else' - then these people aren't going to find your auction.

Also, listing items in the wrong categories is against eBay's rules, and eBay say they will remove any auctions that are wrongly categorised. They don't often actually do this, but it's not worth the risk - especially since breaking any rules can cause them to penalise your account, including losing PowerSeller status if you have it.

So What Can You Do?

Ebay will suggest categories for you when you sell your item, if you type in a few words to describe the item on the category selection page and click 'search'. You can make the best of this feature by typing in exactly what your item is, with brand name and model number (if any), so that eBay can find the best category for you.

If that doesn't work for you, then search yourself for items like yours, and pay attention to which category most of them seem to be in (you can see this near the top of each item's description page). Try different words and see which ones come back with the most results. You can also browse through all the available categories from eBay's front page.

Remember that the more specific the category is, the better - use as many subcategories as are appropriate. Don't just list your HP laptop in the 'Computers' category, for example - list it in 'Computers > Laptops > HP'. Don't worry: your item will still appear in the 'Computers' category, as well as 'Computers > Laptops', because items listed in subcategories are always listed in every category above.

Take some time to look through all the categories and get familiar with the way eBay as a whole is laid out. After all, that's better than getting a few months down the line and finding that you still think of eBay's category system like it's some kind of scary jungle.

What if More Than One Category Fits?

Don't worry, eBay have you covered. For a small extra fee, you can list your item in an extra category, to increase the number of potential buyers who will see it. This isn't always worth it, though - some items only really fit properly in one category, and listing them in extra categories is just a waste.

Once you know where to list your item, the next step is to write your auction's title. The title is the most important thing about your auction - the difference between a good title and a bad title can be the difference between $10 and $100. To learn why this is the case…

13. Ebay Listing Titles

The title that you give your listings and the description that you provide are going to make all the difference when it comes to the sale of your products. The title and the description are your form of advertising in the eBay community.

Without solid titles and strong descriptions you stand the chance of losing buyers to other sellers who stand out in the crowd. Your goal should be to become one of these sellers that stand out in that crowd.

Creating a strong title: Buyers at eBay will notice the product that you're selling from the title that you write for the item. You want to create a title that is immediately eye catching so that buyers want to linger for that crucial extra minute to read your description. Following are some guidelines for writing a strong, eye-catching title:

- Try to use words that are highly descriptive and that fully describe the item that you're selling.
- If appropriate include the key words in the title such as (1) brand names, (2) artist name, (3) designer names, or (4) any other identifying words that you know buyers will recognize.

- You need to precisely say what the item is. Don't be afraid to include the category name in the item title since it never hurts to emphasize this.
- Try to choose words in the title that buyers might use to search for items. This will bring more buyers to your item page.
- You only have so much space for a title so make the most of the words that you use. You don't want to use words that have no meaning, such as "incredible", which really tells the buyer nothing about the item that you're selling.
- Take a look at similar items that sold for a good price. See what titles those sellers used to encourage buyers to read through the description of the item that they were selling.
- There are some types of titles which eBay prohibits the use of. This includes titles that (1) use profane language, (2) use words the lead a buyer to believe the product is "illegal", (3) titles that include phone numbers, email addresses, or URLs, (4) titles that don't adequately describe the item that you're selling in any way.

When you follow these tips you'll be well on your way to creating titles that catch the eyes of buyers.

Creating a strong description: The more time that you put into writing a good description for the items that you're selling, the better chance you have of getting a lot of bids and selling at a high price. A description that is strong and filled with a lot of information will (1) give buyers all that they need to know to want to place a bid on your item, and (2) leave buyers with the impression that you care about what you're selling.

Sellers are always trying new techniques when it comes to item descriptions. Some of the more interesting things that you might want to include in the description are telling the buyer why you personally like the item that you're selling, letting the buyer know what appeals to you about the item, and what use the item might have to anyone who is considering placing a bid.

There are some things that you should include in the description of the products that you're selling. Some of this specific information should include:

- A clear explanation of what the item is.
- What the item is made of and the year that it was made.
- Who created the item, such as artist or author.
- What is the current condition of the item.
- What are the measurements of the item.
- Are there any distinguishing features of the item that the buyer should know about.
- What is the history of the item that you're selling.

There are obviously some pieces of information that you won't be able to include in the item description. Keep in mind that buyers have the ability to get in touch with you if they want to ask for more information.

There are some definite things that you should avoid when it comes to the description of the item. This includes:

- Never include any false information that will deceive a buyer.
- Avoid what is called "keyword spam". This means that you can't include keywords that aren't related to the item

that you're selling, such as throwing in a brand name when you're not selling that particular brand.

Before you finalize your description make sure that you've included all the relevant information. Critical information that you should include:

- Information about your payment methods.
- Information about packaging and shipping.
- Where you're located.
- Any other information that can make the difference between a sale and a non-sale.

As a final note, make sure that check the spelling and grammar of your item descriptions before you submit. Nothing looks more unprofessional than an eBay listing that has spelling and grammar mistakes.

Including Photos in your EBay Listing

To achieve any degree of success as a seller on eBay you'll need to include a picture of the item that you're selling. Buyers are drawn to those listings that have a good, clear photo of the item.

When you're taking a picture of the item there are some basic guidelines that you should follow to make the most of this photo opportunity:

- Make sure that the lighting is good so that you get pictures that are clear and natural. If you're taking a picture outside make sure to use a flash if you need to increase the brightness of the picture.

- Use a backdrop of some kind for smaller items. Try to avoid using a white backdrop as this put too much contrast into the picture.
- Remove other objects from the picture that have no relevance to the item that you're selling.
- Get as close as you can without losing focus.
- Take pictures of sections of the item that you're selling so that buyers can see all sides.
- Take pictures of any distinguishing marks on the item, such as manufacturer stamps on the bottoms of vases.

After you've taken the picture eBay will walk you through the process of uploading the photo to your listing page. When you download the "EBay Picture Services Application" it will be easy for you to manage and upload all your pictures.

You want to develop a design for your online business that is going to enhance your business image and that will add strength to your Internet presence on eBay. This strategy is vital to the success of your business.

Your goal should be to develop a design for your business that you can use in all areas of promoting your online website: advertising through your eBay description, creating strong titles, and including great pictures with your listings. You want to create a business design that will be remembered and recognized by your eBay customers, and that builds trust and reliability in your business as well as consistency.

The way you describe the items that you're selling can make all the difference between a sale or loosing a buyer to another seller. Take some time to learn what works when it comes to item descriptions as well as how you should be designing your listing.

The key to success at eBay is being familiar with the things that work. Most successful sellers have a wide variety of products to sell. They learn to manage their listings effectively and efficiently to make the most out of the quick minute which a buyer spends looking at your listing.

If you want your online business to profit and prosper then you need to become an expert when it comes to the publicity of the items that you have for sale on eBay.

Publicity, or your eBay listing, can earn you a reputation as the expert in your target market, gain the trust and respect of eBay buyers', and in the end earn your business the profits that you need to succeed. Your goal should be to do all of the above without spending thousands of dollars on traditional, and often risky, methods of selling and advertising on the Internet.

EBay is a great online location for you to sell the items that you want to earn money to supplement your income or quit your job and sell at eBay at a full time level.

14. Description Writing Techniques

Once you've drawn the buyers in with your title, the next thing to do is to tell them all about your item with the description. But just what should you write in your description?

At its heart, your item description is an ad. Without making it too obvious, you should be writing sales copy. You're trying to get buyers excited about your products, and that's usually hard - but on eBay, if you have the right thing to sell and give enough details, the buyers almost excite themselves.

Technical Details

Include every technical detail you know, including the item's manufacturer, its condition, how big it is, where and when it was made, its history, and anything else special about it. Don't be too boring, though: the best descriptions are written in friendly, conversational language, and show a real knowledge of the item. Whatever you do, make sure you tell the truth!

Remember that most of the people who'll be buying your item will be just as knowledgeable about it as you are, if not more - this is their hobby, and they're experts. Don't feel like you need to explain the basics of the item: just go into as much technical detail as you can. As a rule, don't write anything in the description if you don't know what it means, as the chances are someone will, and if you've got it slightly wrong then you'll look like you don't know what you're talking about.

Interesting Details

You might find that you enjoy writing a few things about how you got the item, why you're selling it, and who you think might like it. This isn't strictly necessary, but it gives your auctions some character and a personal touch, and can make people more likely to trust you.

People might wonder what you're doing selling 500 CDs all at once, and if you tell them the reason, then they'll feel reassured that nothing dodgy is going on. If you're selling them because you're having a baby and you need the space, just say so.

Write as Much as You Can

Leave nothing out of your description, even if that seems to you like it makes it cumbersomely long. There is no way you can be too thorough: someone, somewhere will appreciate that you took the time to write the extra information.

Don't assume that anyone who wants extra information will email you to ask a question: many buyers are shy and won't do it. Think of questions that buyers might have and add the answers to your description, as people generally tend to ask the same questions over and over again.

Each time a buyer does email you with a question, you should both answer their question and update your description so that it will include the answer next time. If people ask questions that are answered in the description, try putting these parts of the auction on a line alone, or in bold, to make them easier to notice.

15. Increasing Responses

So you've got the buyer in front of your auction, and they've read the description. They're must be interested, or they wouldn't be looking… but just how can you push them over that line and make them leave a bid? Read on for some tips.

Improve your picture: In all that description writing, you might have missed the vital importance of your item's picture. A picture with bad lighting or an intrusive background looks amateurish and won't make anyone want to buy from you.

Add an About Me page: You'll be surprised how much you can reassure bidders just by creating an About Me page and putting a little bit about yourself on your business on there. You can also have a few special offers there for people who bother to look at the page, and let people subscribe to your mailing list so that you can email them updates.

Use SquareTrade: Signing up at SquareTrade and displaying their logo on your auctions shows that you are committed to have them resolve any disputes that arise. You always see this on PowerSellers auctions - it makes you look more professional.

Write terms and conditions: Have the 'small print' clearly visible on all your auctions, giving details of things like shipping times and prices, your refund policy, and any other business practices you might have. This helps build confidence with buyers.

Show off your feedback: Copy and paste a selection of the feedback comments you're most proud of to each item's description page, instead of making bidders go and look for it. If you have 100% positive feedback, be sure to write that on every auction too.

Add NR to your titles: If you have extra space in a title, put 'NR' (no reserve) on the end. Bidders prefer auctions that don't have a reserve price, and doing this lets them see that yours don't.

Benefits not features: Make sure your description focuses on the benefits that your item can give to the customer, not just its features. This is a classic sales technique. If you have trouble with this, remember: 'cheap' is a feature, 'save money' is a benefit.

List more items: If you want more people to respond to your items, then list more items! You might find you have better like listing items at the same time, instead of one-by-one. There's no need to use a Dutch auction - you can just keep two or three auctions going at once for an item you have more than one of in stock.

Buy some upgrades: The best upgrade is the most expensive one, which makes your item appear first in search results. In crowded categories, you might find that this is worth the money.

Once you've got some buyers, you want to keep them coming back to you!

16. Rules for Selling

There are several rules that you should be aware of so that you don't make any crucial mistakes when it comes to selling your items on eBay. Although the process of selling on eBay is as simple as possible there are still some things that you should know before you start selling and growing your business.

One of the most important things that you need to be aware of is keeping your selling and buying transactions as safe and secure as possible. There are policies in place which ensure the safety and privacy of the financial information of the people who are buying from you as well as your own financial information. Some of the other things that you'll need to know when you sell on eBay include:

- EBay's tax policy and regulations.
- The policies for listing at eBay.
- How to sell your items internationally.

Tax policy: When you sell on eBay you need make sure that you observe all of the taxes that are applicable to the sale. This includes domestic tax laws, international tax laws, any local statutes, and any ordinances. When you sell on eBay you are committing the act of listing, soliciting, and selling certain items. These items and the selling practice are liable to fees and taxes.

Policy violations: There are some types of polices that are not allowed on eBay. It's important that you are aware of these polices so that you don't find yourself in violation of the rules. The last thing that you want is to face a temporary suspension because you weren't aware of a certain policy. These violations include:

- Shill bidding is not allowed on eBay.
- You may not solicit your items off the eBay website while you are soliciting them on eBay.
- You cannot, on your own, interrupt a transaction that is already in process.

If buyers, or other sellers, find that you are in violation of any of the rules and regulations that eBay clearly outlines they can file what is called a "trading offence" with eBay administration. As well, if you find that any other sellers are in violation of these policies you can file an offence.

Trading offence: If you want to file a trading offence against another seller you need to follow this procedure:

- Read once again the policy page at eBay which clearly outlines the policies that must be followed. Make sure that the eBay user is in violation of one of these policies. There is a link on this webpage which you can use to send a report directly to eBay.
- Fill in the report with all the required information that eBay will need to make a decision about the trading offence. This report information should include any

emails that are connected with the offence, as well as subject lines that are clear and easy to understand.

- Only file a trading offence report once. The more times that you report an offence the slower the process will move as eBay administrators need to read each report and add it to the file.

EBay will investigate all trading offence that are filed and will make a decision based on the circumstances. Some of the actions that eBay may take to deal with trading offences are a warning, a temporary suspension, or a permanent suspension.

17. EBay Storefronts

EBay Store Fronts are another way that you can sell items on eBay. The products that you choose to sell will have a front row seat to eBay buyers who are looking for the items that you're offering.

EBay is one advertising opportunity that you might not want to miss so that you can maximize your business exposure on the Internet. When you use an eBay Store Front you can connect with thousands of people every day who shop on eBay.

It costs very little for you to open an eBay Store. For just a low cost each month you can start to boost your Internet presence, increase your sales, and add to your customer database. When you start an eBay Store you'll have these tools at your disposal:

- An online Store Front that is completely yours to develop and create to fit your business needs.
- Tracking methods and a way to analyze how your business is doing within the eBay community.
- Easy tools to manage the running of your eBay Store.
- Tools at hand for marketing and merchandising your product.

There are many benefits of an eBay Store Front. When you open an eBay Store Front you'll find that there are many benefits to you and your business. An eBay Store Front gives you the opportunity to reach thousands of people each day and increase the exposure that you need to obtain more customers.

One of the big benefits of having an eBay Store Front is that it gives your website a look of professionalism that is going to give you the credibility that you need to reach customers that are looking for a particular product or service on the Internet.

It takes only a few minutes to start your eBay store, which means that you'll be up and running in no time, and ready for customers to find you.

You'll be able to customize your Store Front to the exact design that you feel best stylizes the products that you're selling.

There are over 20 different design categories that you can choose from when you sign up with eBay Store Front. And you'll be able to have a unique address on the Internet for your Store Front so that customers can find you fast and easily, book marking your Store Front website so that they can return again later for repeat sales and to find out what's new in your Store.

Each month you'll have access to a variety of reports that will let you know exactly how you're doing. Some of the data information that you'll receive each month includes:

- Traffic report: traffic reports so that you know how many web visitors are stopping by your eBay Store Front.
- Sales report: sales reports, to let you know how many sales your Store Front has generated.

- Accounting information: accounting information that you can use to export your PayPal and eBay sales transactions into accounting software programs such as QuickBooks or your own Excel spreadsheet.

When it comes to the promotion of your eBay Store Front you won't be left in the cold, since eBay will give you all the help that you need to bring customers to your eBay Store. EBay will list your Store Front on all the appropriate listings within their website pages as well as send out marketing correspondence to your customers.

When you sign up with eBay Store Front you'll have a search engine in the content of your store. This means that your customers will be able to use this search tool to find the products, or services, that you're selling.

You'll save a lot of time using the eBay Store Front to sell your products and spend more time concentrating on your business and other marketing strategies.

When you sign up with eBay Store Front you'll see a definite increase in your sales and profits, as well as watch your customer database grow and turn into repeat sales.

Top Selling Items

EBay listings include all kinds of items for sale, from the plain and ordinary to the wild and amazing. You will have to determine what types of items you want to sell. There are some things you may want to consider before you make your decision.

Are you going to be selling items that you already have around your home? Or are you going to find products in your local area that you are going to purchase with the intent of reselling the item and making a profit?

To give you an idea of what is being sold at eBay here are a few of the items offered for sale today:

- Collectibles: There are a wide range of collectibles that are sold every day on eBay. From the traditional fare of stamps, coins, and comic books to the more specialized items such as Beanie Babies™, Zippo™ lighters, and PEZ™ dispensers, eBay is by far the number one place on the Web to find the widest range of both popular and hard-to-find collectable items.

- Electronics: EBay is an excellent source to sell both new and used electronic items. Whether you are selling individual items or lots that have been purchased in bulk, there are always buyers for electronic goods of all shapes and sizes. Cell phones, stereo equipment, computers, and video games are just a few of the millions of high tech gadgetry that can be found across many sections of the eBay community.

- Antiques: Items in this category include everything from Asian vases to antique maps. If you are considering selling an antique make sure you know the value of the item so that you can verify the item's worth. If you have any documentation that legitimizes the age and antique value of the item you should make note of this in your item listing. Take a photo of any documentation that supports the value and age of the antique you are selling.

You should also take a picture of any identifying marks on the antique to establish its worth. The more information you can provide potential buyers the more successful you will be with the sale.

- Books: Books are a very popular sale item on eBay. Sub-categories include children's books, poetry, reference books, and the latest fiction. If you are thinking about selling books at eBay you will have to do your research very carefully to make certain that you are selling at a competitive market value.

  One of the best things about selling books is that they are easy to package and ship to the seller. Books are relatively difficult to damage during mailing and shipping costs will be minimal compared to the shipping expenses of larger, more fragile items bought on eBay. You will want to find out the availability of a certain book you are thinking about selling.

  If the book is readily available through other selling markets, such as bookstores and supermarkets, there may not be a high demand for the book and you may want to reconsider spending time listing it on eBay. Make sure the books you are selling are in good condition. If there is wear and tear or damage to the book be sure to make mention of this in your eBay listing. You want to give the buyer as much information as possible.

- DVDs and Movies: DVDs and movies are a great item to sell on eBay. Be sure to include information such as media format (DVD/VHS/Beta/Laserdisc/etc) and encoding information (such as PAL/NTSC). When dealing with box sets, be sure to include bonus items and packaging details.

- Arts and Crafts: On eBay you will find many examples of the modern "cottage industry" with individuals and small "mom and pop" operations who create arts and crafts of every flavor imaginable.

  From homemade candles to home fired ceramics to hand strung beads and artwork, eBay has no shortage of merchandise that caters to those who desire items with that "personal touch". In addition to offering the final products of many creative individuals, eBay also hosts many vendors of arts and crafts supplies.

There are some items that you are prohibited to sell on eBay.

EBay will end your listing if you violate their policy of what you can not sell. As well as items that you are prohibited from selling, some items may be considered questionable (can only be listed under certain conditions) or potentially infringing (item may be in violation of certain copyrights). There are some of the items that you are prohibited from selling on eBay:

- Alcohol
- Counterfeit items
- Firearms, Ammunition, Replicas, and Militaria
- Drugs and drug paraphernalia

- Plants and seeds
- Stocks and other securities
- Lottery tickets
- Stolen property

The list of items to sell on eBay is endless. If you do your research well you will be able to make an informative decision about what you are going to sell on eBay to make money. Experiment with different items to see what you enjoy selling and at which you are most successful.

Finding Items to Sell

There are many places for PowerSellers to find items to sell, and make a profit from, on eBay. With a little bit of research and as little as 4 or 5 hours a week, you too can find yourself running a successful e-business using eBay as your marketing vehicle and e-commerce engine.

Here are some suggestions for where to begin searching for merchandise for sale on eBay which can result in the highest profit margins and therefore more money in YOUR pocket:

- Flea markets. It is possible to find many hidden treasures at flea markets in your local area. It is common for attics to be cleared out and surplus stock from a variety of retail outlets to be emptied into the flea market ecosystem in the hopes of making at least some amount of money from what is considered to be "surplus" or "salvaged". It is here that you can find the best deals, but you can also uncover hard-to-find collectables, electronics, and many other categories of merchandise that are ripe for the picking for resale on eBay. Another thing to look out for when scouring flea markets is geographically-specific items.

Items which may be hard to find in one part of the world may be very easy to find in another. Due to the fact that eBay is a global market, it can pay off very well to keep your eyes peeled for these little nuggets of profit.

- EBay itself. Another great place to find the types of things to resell on eBay is right there on eBay. Although at first thought it may seem a little counterproductive, what it all really boils down to is getting a good deal at a good time. Try to focus on types of merchandise you have more than a cursory knowledge of.

  For example, if you are a comic book buff who has been collecting for years, you will have a great eye for that particular subsection of eBay (and a much greater chance of knowing a good deal when you see it). Of particular focus should be auctioneers letting go of entire lots of merchandise for events like estate sales, unclaimed freight, or store closings. Digging through eBay's mountain of merchandise when you know what you are doing can prove not only profitable, but a lot of fun as well.

- Swap meets/conventions. It can also pay to take note when your local area is hosting special interest conventions and swap meets, such as gun shows, comic book conventions and the like. With a little research on eBay regarding the current market for the particular classes of merchandise focused on at these meets, studious, and diligent individuals can profit greatly from very little initial investment.

In addition to the diverse collections of various types of items that these meets and conventions will place at your fingertips, you can also usually acquire a lot of freebies (or schwag, in convention nomenclature), which can be easily resold to enthusiasts of the particular subject you are participating in the meet for.

- Buying in bulk. This is less of a "where" and more of a "how", but it's definitely applicable: It seems like a lot of PowerSellers find something they get a good bargain on locally and sell it to a wide market that doesn't have that same access. For instance, you might discover that computer desk shelves are selling on eBay for quite a bit more than your local bulk retailer charges.

  This is an excellent opportunity for you to profit from your location and what you have access to. To take this another step further you may wish to contact the manufacturer and find a wholesaler to purchase it in bulk.

  Some manufacturers will work with you in this way and some won't, you'll just have to experiment and find out. Another good idea is visiting closeout stores and outlets. It's a pot luck selection that sells for way below catalogue price, and eBay sellers are looking to make the profit margin from people who don't have access to these stores.

- Clearance racks at malls. Try searching the clearance racks in your local shopping malls for great deals on clothing. Many people live in areas that are not serviced by shopping malls and therefore don't have access to the types of merchandise that you do.

It's a good idea to visit these stores during big sales, especially right after the holiday period or at the turn of seasons when retailers will be trying to get rid of their old stock to make room for the new. Particularly focus on trendy stores that deal in expensive brand name items. Often you will be able to find very popular, trendy labels for a fraction of their retail cost, sometimes even below cost.

- Garage Sales. Don't forget to check your local paper for garage/lawn sales. Usually you can find great deals if you are willing to dig and sift through a few garage sales every weekend.

- Your own attic. You would be shocked what some people, and maybe even YOU, have in the attic. The next time you do some spring cleaning, be sure to take the time to dig through some of those boxes, wooden chests, and foot lockers collecting dust in your attic, basement or storage shed. Anything from antiques to unique collectables can be found by just digging around bit a rainy April afternoon.

18. Wholesale Tips

If you want to have a profitable online business selling products on eBay you'll need have a constant source of items to sell. Rather than finding items to sell at garage sales and flea markets you'll want to establish relationships with wholesalers who are selling items that you're interested in selling.

There are several ways that you can find the right wholesaler for you:

- Wholesale lots: You can find wholesale lots on the eBay website so that almost all the searching for products is done for you. There are many categories that are listed featuring almost any type of product imaginable. This includes electronics, books, collectibles, music, clothing, and household items.

  Take some time to do your own buyer search on eBay to find out what items that are listed are popular. Then you can focus on a similar product so that you can sell at competitive prices. When you find a wholesale product that you want to sell you can sell it for a considerable profit on eBay. The important thing to do is thoroughly research the market on eBay before you decide on what products to sell.

- Storage unit auctions: Another great way to find products to sell on eBay is by finding out when storage unit businesses are having an auction. Most storage unit businesses will auction several times each year to get rid of unwanted items that have been unclaimed for a certain period of time.

  This is a great way for you pick up some cheap items that you can resell for a great profit. The items that you know won't sell on eBay can be given away to charity or you can hold your own garage sale to make a penny or two.

- Search the Internet: The Internet is a great way to find wholesalers that have some great products for you to sell online at eBay. Type a keyword such as wholesaler, liquidator, or wholesale trading into any search engine and you'll be rewarded with a huge listing of wholesalers from around the world.

- Wholesale directories: You can find wholesalers by looking in a wholesale directory. You can find a directory on the Internet. You'll be able to find lists of distributors, manufacturers, and wholesalers in well formatted categories that make it easy for you to find what you're looking for.

- Exporters and importers: If you're looking at the big picture, and plan on selling a wide variety of items on eBay, you may want to contact those companies that specialize in imports from overseas.

- Local wholesalers: Look for wholesalers where you live since there are usually many sources available locally. You want to find one or more wholesalers from who you can purchase the items that you know you can sell on eBay. A local wholesaler will save you money on shipping costs and you'll be able to supplement your inventory at any time without the wait of shipping.

When you're looking for a wholesaler it's important to find one or more that specialize in the products that you're interested in. If you've done your research on eBay you should already know which items are current hot sales and which ones aren't.

Another thing to remember when you're looking for a wholesaler is that the fewer people are already buying from the wholesaler the more unique your product will be when you sell it on eBay. Take some time to find products that are one of a kind, such as a craft item that is rare to find.

19. Building a PowerSeller Reputation

The absolute most critical element to the eBay selling experience is building your eBay PowerSeller reputation. The basic component of the reputation system on eBay is user feedback.

For every eBay transaction, including auctions and "Buy it now" transactions, both parties involved in the deal will have an opportunity to assign a positive, neutral, or negative score to their transaction, as well as provide textual comments. Here's how eBay describes the feedback system on their website:

"Every eBay user has a feedback score based on ratings from other members. Feedback lets you reward eBay users and inform the community about your experiences with others. Typically, members give a positive rating if they are happy with a transaction and a negative when basic obligations have not been met. Keep in mind that what you say about other members becomes a permanent part of their eBay reputation."

In order to be successful in any capacity on eBay, whether you are buying or selling, it will be necessary to develop a positive PowerSeller reputation within the eBay community by embodying sound business practices and good customer relations. Here are a few suggestions to get you started:

- Keep clear and open channels of communication with your customers. Make sure you answer questions from potential bidders in a timely manner and be particularly mindful to field any inquiries from auction winners. Being quick to respond to perceived problems can mean the difference between a positive and a negative feedback which can and will be a direct influence on potential buyers out there.

- Participate in as many transactions as possible. Besides your feedback ratio, potential buyers will also give some scrutiny to the sheer volume of business you do. If given the choice of doing business with two individual sellers, and one of those sellers has a tried and true reputation with thousands of transactions, the buyer is most likely going to go with the seller that has the most experience. That seller should be you.

- Be open and honest. Being the most communicative PowerSeller on eBay is no good if you are being misleading or dishonest with your customers. It is imperative that you take every step possible to ensure that you're being as honest as you can be with your clientele. If you are selling an item that may have perceivable flaws, it is a good idea to make sure that that is clear in the item summary.

  Be sure to be up front regarding your shipping costs and any other fees that may be incurred above and beyond the winning bid on the item. Never participate in questionable, sneaky practices such as profiting from shipping costs by padding the final shipping and handling price.

While trickery like that may make you a little extra in the short term, you will end up paying for it in negative feedback and/or bad word-of-mouth from dissatisfied customers.

Powerful Selling Techniques

There are many things you can do to increase the sale of your items on eBay. Not only do you need to register on eBay and create a seller's account, you need to use all the techniques and tips at your fingertips to see consistent and increased sales.

Here are some general techniques for you to consider, some of which have been touched on in other chapters as well as here:

- Treat your buyer's right. It is very important to build up a good relationship with your buyers and potential buyers. Be sure to answer all e-mail questions as well as you can. Make sure that you leave positive feedback for buyers. This is an important step towards building up your reputation as a PowerSeller on eBay.

- Do not expect "instant wealth". If you start selling with the intent of becoming rich instantly you may be disappointed to find that earning a substantial profit selling on eBay takes some time and effort. You need to build up your eBay business over a period of several months. If you are consistent and determined you will quickly see the results in your bank account.

- Remember that selling on eBay is a business. If you keep that in mind you will treat it with more seriousness.
- Learn how to stand out from the crowd of other sellers on eBay.

- Offer as many payment options as possible, including credit cards. The more payment options you offer prospective buyers, the more bidders your product will attract and the more successful your selling on eBay will be.

- Be knowledgeable about your shipping options. Offer as many options as you can, especially for international buyers. Be VERY clear when outlining your shipping policies for bidders.

- Be sure to write very descriptive listings for your merchandise. As much care should be taken in articulating the sale in words as there is to the photograph of your item.

- Constantly check out what the competition is doing. Make time to see what your competitors are selling and at what prices. You need to remain up-to-date so that you can remain competitive.

- Participate in the eBay online community areas. This includes the message boards and chat areas.

- Include measurements for any merchandise in which the dimensions or weight can be an issue.
- If you are going to be selling a LOT of items, consider opening an EBay store.

- Maintain a professional attitude. As with any other sector of the business world, a good professional attitude and a professional reputation will take you far.

- Keep track of all your sales records for tax purposes.

- Keep a database of your customers. Make sure you record business-critical information such as shipping address and contact information.

Finances: Try to keep your personal and business financial accounts as separate as possible. You want to have accurate records of your spending and profits from your eBay business without having them cross over to the other.

You'll need to record all of your expenses and your income when they happen rather than when the cash leaves or comes into your hand.

This type of an accounting system is called "accrual" accounting and is much more accurate than "cash" accounting where the transactions are only recorded when the cash actually changes hands between you and the buyer or you and the wholesaler.

You need to be honest about the changes in your income level. It's your legal responsibility to record any increase in income on your taxes.

It will be your responsibility to record and report the taxes that you owe. EBay won't accept any of the blame for any taxes that you fail to record and pay.

Permits and licenses: You'll need to contact a Customs and Excise office to register your new business and apply for an export permit if you're going to be selling your products internationally.

You'll also need to apply for a license to sell food products on the Internet. Make sure that you find out about all the permits and licenses you need in the area where you live to make sure that you have everything that you need to legally sell on eBay.

It's important that you accurately describe what it is that you're selling so that you don't misrepresent the item.

Selling Issues to Avoid
Of course, in dealing with online auctions there are many things you can do to improve your business.

But in addition to all of the things you can do to make business better, there are also things that you should NOT do if you want to be a PowerSeller on eBay.

There are some things that will gain you no benefit and can even HURT your business on eBay. Here is a short list of what NOT to do:

- Don't use music, big gaudy graphics, or other animations or a multicolored background in your listing.

- Don't rush to leave negative feedback for a non-paying bidder.
- Don't delay in shipping your items.
- Don't try to make a profit off of "handling charges".
- Don't use "As is" as a description in your listings.
- Don't wait for the buyer to leave feedback first.
- Don't fail to identify defects in your merchandise.
- Don't list your auctions so they end on a Holiday.
- Don't be afraid to accept international buyers.
- Don't make threats or use a negative tone in your listing.

20. Ebay Tools & Resources

There are many software tools out there that can help you make the most out of the eBay experience.

From sniping software to data analysis to auction tools, you will find many useful utilities exist on the web to make your powerselling auctions more efficient and effective. Here are some examples of software you will find useful:

- Baycheck is a utility that allows quick access to a TON of user information. Using Baycheck, everything you need to know about a user is just a click away, like: Seller history, bidder history, feedback received, and feedback left.

- DeepAnalysis is eBay research software. Using DeepAnalysis eBay users can extract and analyze licensed eBay data and statistics for any eBay market sector, then use DeepAnalysis to reveal market trends and develop eBay strategies that will help you make money on eBay.

- Turbo Sniper provides: Auction sniping, standalone and server-based auction tracking, email automation, bulk search and data extraction, and universal automation and analysis.

- Bidnapper is another sniping tool.

- AuctionSleuth is combination sniping and buy-it-now bidding software that can help you find good deals on eBay.

Final Words

You are now ready to begin earning money by becoming a PowerSeller on eBay! The advice, suggestions, tools, and techniques presented to you in these chapters will have prepared you for what to expect when selling at eBay.

Ebay will guide you through the process of becoming an online PowerSeller. Their website is packed with help and will answer any other questions you have about selling on eBay. Make sure to take advantage of their help section.

In this day and age we are all looking for ways to supplement our income so that we can save a little money for something special or to help pay our bills and debts. By selling on eBay you can earn that money without giving up your other job. You can work in the comfort of your own home so you don't have to worry about travel costs. You can spend time with your family while still earning money.

It won't take long before you start to see a substantial increase in the sale of your items when you follow the information that is outlined in this book. Whether you are selling items you already have in your home or whether you are buying items specifically for the purpose of resale, eBay provides you with the virtual Internet space to connect with buyers from all walks of life.

After reading this book you will have an edge over other sellers and will have the knowledge to build a successful Internet business for yourself. You will soon find yourself reaping the rewards and benefits that come from being an eBay PowerSeller!

We hope you have found this book useful. If you do your research carefully and keep organized, there is no limit to the money you can make selling on eBay. Sometimes it can be a little difficult to get started, but persistence and discipline will pay off in the end. There are all sorts of great reasons to start making money from selling on eBay today.

Besides the potential to make a lot of profit, you will get to make your own hours and generally be your own boss, which is great. So give it a try today, you'll be glad you did.

Now, as the Nike commercial says, Just Do It!

Ebay Glossary

Bid: telling eBay's system the maximum price you are prepared to pay for an item.

Dutch: an auction where more than one of an item is available.

Feedback: positive or negative comments left about other users on eBay.

Mint: in perfect condition.

Non-paying bidder: a bidder who wins an auction but does not then go on to buy the item.

PayPal: an electronic payment method accepted by most sellers.

Rare: used and abused on eBay, now entirely meaningless.

Reserve: the minimum price the seller will accept for the item.

Shill bid: a fake bid placed by a seller trying to drive up their auction's price.

Snail Mail: the post, which is obviously very slow compared to email.

Sniping: bidding at the last second to win the item before anyone else can outbid you.

Initials & Abbreviations

AUD: Australian Dollar Currency.

BIN: Buy it Now. A fixed price auction.

BNWT: Brand New With Tags. An item that has never been used and still has its original tags.

BW: Black and White. Used for films, photos etc.

CONUS: Continental United States. Generally used by sellers who don't want to post things to Alaska or Hawaii.

EUR: Euro Currency.

FC: First Class. Type of postage.

GBP: Great British Pounds Currency.

HTF: Hard To Find. Not quite as abused as 'rare', but getting there.

NIB: New in Box. Never opened, still in its original box.

NR: No Reserve. An item where the seller has not set a reserve price.

OB: Original Box. An item that has its original box (but might have been opened).

PM: Priority Mail.

PP: Parcel Post.

SH: Shipping and Handling. The fees the buyer will pay you for postage.

USD: United States Dollars Currency.

VGC: Very Good Condition. Not mint, but close.

www.ingramcontent.com/pod-product-compliance
Lightning Source LLC
Chambersburg PA
CBHW071223220526
45468CB00002B/705